Acting
with Luke

by

D. B. Livingston

ACKNOWLEDGMENTS

I would like to thank Dan Hummel for his technical support, Lori Bergeron for her editing and, our daughter, Laura DeFilippo, for her photography. I would also like to thank our grandson, Luke, for taking time out of his busy schedule to be on the cover photo with Grandpa. And, I would especially like to thank the Lord Jesus Christ for saving me from my sins and calling me to be a pastor and a writer.

Act 1

Dr. Luke begins his second book, like the first, with an introduction to his dear "friend of God," Theophilus, whom we know little about. However, back in Luke 1:3, the good doctor calls him "most excellent Theophilus," leading most commentators to believe he was probably a high-ranking government official. I love it: "The Doctor and the Politician!"

Luke tells Theophilus and us, in Act 1:1 and 2, that his first account (the gospel of Luke) was "about all that Jesus began to do and teach (from the time He was 12 in the temple), until the day when He was taken up to heaven, after He had given orders to the apostles whom He had chosen."

In Act 1:3, Luke gives us some additional information of the time Jesus had with the apostles following His resurrection, writing, "To these (the apostles) He also presented Himself alive after His suffering, by many convincing proofs, appearing to them over a period of 40 days and speaking of the things concerning the kingdom of God." Wow! It just dawned on me that Jesus spent 40 days in the wilderness (Luke 4:1, 2) before He began His ministry and now, the same amount of time at the end of His ministry. Go figure!

Notice, in Act 1:3, Jesus is talking with His Jewish friends about "the kingdom of God" which I am sure, as Jews, they were all excited about. Then, in verses 4 and 5, He tells them to wait in Jerusalem until they were "baptized with the Holy Spirit." Earlier, in John 14:16-26 and 16:5-15, He did say something to them about the Holy Spirit coming upon them and reminding them of the things He had taught them. I am thinking they had no idea what that meant, but would soon find out.

Next, we read in verse 6, "So when they had come together, they were asking Him, saying, 'Lord, is it at this time You are restoring the kingdom to Israel?" Keep in mind, the apostles were Jews who, now that their King/Messiah had come, were hoping His glorious "kingdom" would come on earth as it is in heaven (Matthew 6:10)."

Jesus being Jesus, said to them, in verse 7, "It is not for you to know the times or epochs (seasons, KJV) which the Father has fixed by His own authority; but you will receive power when the Holy Spirit has come upon you; and you shall be my witnesses (martus in the Greek from which we get the word "martyr") both in Jerusalem, and in all Judea and Samaria, and even to the remotest part of the earth."

Now, I wasn't there but, for some unknown reason, Luke did not record any of the apostles' reaction to what Jesus had just said. I am thinking, they must have been somewhat disappointed because their King had come, but not with the kingdom. When He said to them, "and you shall be My witnesses in Jerusalem (where the Jews had conspired with the Romans to crucify Jesus), Judea (a Roman province), Samaria (where the enemies of the Jews lived) and even to the remotest parts of the earth, I could be wrong, but I can just hear them thinking, "He's got to be kidding!"

Luke very casually records in verse 9,

"And after He had said these things, He was lifted up while they were looking on, and a cloud received Him out of their sight." Wow! Talk about a new experience with Jesus! In verse 10, the good doctor records, "And as they were gazing intently into the sky while He was going (perhaps hoping He would make a U-turn and come back with the kingdom), behold, two men in white clothing stood beside them." This was like, as Yogi Berra once said, "Dejavu all over again!"

You may remember, back in Luke 24:1-3, when some of the women who had followed Jesus, went to the tomb to anoint His body, they noticed the stone had been rolled away from the tomb, but He wasn't in the tomb. In verses 4-7, Luke wrote, "While they were perplexed about this, two men suddenly stood near them in dazzling clothing; and as the women were terrified and bowed their faces to the ground, the men said to them, 'Why do you seek the living among the dead? He is not here, but He has risen. Remember how He spoke to you while He was still in Galilee, saying that the Son of Man must be delivered into the hands of sinful men, and be crucified, and the third day rise again.' And they remembered His words."

How cool was that! First, the women who had come to the tomb to anoint Jesus' body, saw two male angels dressed in white who asked them a question. And now, after Jesus' ascension to heaven, the apostles saw two male angels dressed in white who also asked them a question!

Note: Whenever angels appear in Scripture, they are always men. In addition to the two passages above, angels also appear as men in Genesis 18, 19 and Daniel 9:21. Some might ask, "What about the two women 'with the wind beneath their wings' in Zechariah 5:9?" Charles Ryrie comments: "They are either agents of God or forces of evil." I am leaning towards "the forces of evil," as the context is that these two women were "taking an ephah (measure of grain), representing "wickedness" (verse 8) to build a temple in the land of Shinar or Babylon (verse 11).

I find it very interesting, but not surprising, that most angels I have seen in stores, homes and on Christmas trees are either children or women. So, I wonder, "Is this another one of the devil's schemes to confuse people about the truth of God's Word." What do you think?

Let me show you one more interesting thing in Act 1, verse 12. Luke records: "Then they returned to Jerusalem from the mount called Olivet (Mt. of Olives), which is near Jerusalem, a Sabbath's day journey away."

Back in verse 11, the angels said to the apostles, "This Jesus, who has been taken up from you into heaven, will come in just the same way as you have watched Him go into heaven." We just read, in the previous paragraph, that Jesus ascended to heaven from the Mt. of Olives.

Now, turn with me back to Zechariah 14 which describes the second coming of Christ to the earth to reign as King. Let's look at verses 1-4a (the "a" means the first part of the verse). Zechariah the prophet records: "Behold, a day is coming for the Lord when the spoil taken from you will be divided among you. For I will gather all nations to Jerusalem for battle (Armageddon), and the city (Jerusalem) will be captured, the houses plundered, the women ravished and half of the city exiled, but the rest of the people will not be cut off from the city. Then the Lord will go forth and fight against those nations, as when He fights on a day of battle. In that day His feet will stand on the Mt. of Olives, which is in front of Jerusalem on the east."

Did you get that? The angels told the men that Jesus would return to the exact same place from which he left which was the Mt. of Olives! I call this "Back to the Future" for the angels' prophecy in Acts 1:12 will be fulfilled in Zechariah 14:4!

Okay, let's move on. The 11 apostles have now returned to Jerusalem. Luke then records in Act 1, verse 13, "When they entered the city; they went up to the upper room where they were staying." Wow! I just read something I had never seen before. I knew that the apostles met with Jesus in the "upper room," but I never realized they had stayed there.

Thank You, Holy Spirit, for showing me something new!

The next verse (14) is a favorite of mine. Why? Because the good doctor tells us: "These all (the 11 apostles) with one mind were continually devoting themselves to prayer, along with the women, and Mary, the mother of Jesus, and with His brothers." I am not surprised by the fact that the 11 were there, along with the women who followed Jesus and Mary, His mother, because they were all believers in Him. I was pleasantly surprised to learn that Jesus' brothers were now with the group in the upper room. Why? Because, back in John 7:5, we read, "For not even His brothers were believing in Him." Talk about unsaved loved ones! I am sure their mother was among those who were praying for their salvation. Her prayer was answered when they finally believed in Jesus as their Savior! Glory to God! A good reminder that we should only speak truth in love (Ephesians 4:15) to our unsaved loved ones when they are open to hear the Truth. If they are not open to hearing the Truth, then we are to love and pray for them and leave the rest up to God.

In John 21:15-17, Jesus asked Peter three times, "Do you love me?" And, each time, Peter expressed his love for Jesus. After each of Peter's expressions of love for His Master, Jesus gave him three charges: "Tend My lambs, Shepherd My sheep and Tend My sheep." Note: As a pastor for over 40 years, I see these charges as the main responsibilities of the pastor: 1. Tending or feeding (KJV) Jesus' lambs or baby Christians on the truth of God's Word. 2. Shepherding or taking care of the whole flock of sheep. 3. Tending or feeding the whole flock. In other words, the pastor is to be a shepherd of sheep, teaching them and taking care of their needs to the glory of God. Now Peter was ready to lead the group.

One of the first things Peter needed to do as the leader of the group was to choose another man to replace Judas, quoting from Psalm 109:8, "Let another take his office." Note: Again, I am amazed at how well Peter, the former fisherman, knew the Hebrew Scriptures. Luke then records, in verses 21 and

22, Peter listing the qualifications for a candidate to succeed Judas: "Therefore it is necessary that of the men who have accompanied us all the time that the Lord Jesus went in and out among us – beginning with the baptism of John until the day He was taken up from us – one of these must become a witness with us of His resurrection." Note: There are some believers in Jesus who think Paul should have been the 12th apostle, except for the fact he was not with Jesus at His baptism, resurrection and ascension.

In verse 23, Luke tells us that the 11 put forward two men: Joseph Barsabbas (son of Saba) who was also called Justus, and Matthias. Don't you just love it how Luke tells us Joseph's nickname was "Justus!" Next, in verse 24, we learn the apostles prayed, "You, Lord, who know the hearts of all men, show which one of these two You have chosen to occupy the ministry and apostleship from which Judas turned aside to go to his own place." Then, we read, in verse 26, "And they drew lots for them, and the lot fell to Matthias; and he was added to the eleven apostles." Now, they were once again, a complete group of 12.

Now, maybe you're thinking, "Why did they cast lots to determine the outcome?" I like Charles Ryrie's explanation: "The occasion was unique, for the Lord was not there in person to appoint and the Spirit had not yet been given in the special way of Pentecost." This also makes me think back to Proverbs 16:33 where Solomon wrote: "The lot is cast into the lap, but its every decision is from the Lord." As I have said in a previous book, "We vote, but God decides the outcome!" Oh, if only we, as Christians, would accept that, then thank God for His decision, move on and not only pray for our leaders (regardless of their party affiliation), as we are called to do in I Timothy 2:1-4, but also honor (value) them, as we are called to do in I Peter 2:17.

Act 2

Dr. Luke begins this chapter, in verses 1 and 2, by telling us it was the day of Pentecost, one of the three yearly Jewish festivals, when the Jews would go up to Jerusalem to celebrate and give thanks to God for blessing them with the first fruits of the harvest. Luke tells us that the twelve "were all together in one place and suddenly there came from heaven a noise like a violent rushing wind, and it filled the whole house where they were sitting."

What happens next, in verse 3, is truly amazing: "And there appeared to them tongues as of fire distributing themselves and resting on each one of them." Now, I might have said in a previous book, "If there is a DVD library in heaven, I would first like to see the creation." What about you? What would you like to see? What happened next with the apostles would be a good one to see as well.

Luke writes, in verses 4-6, "And they were all filled with the Holy Spirit and began to speak with other tongues, as the Spirit was giving them utterance. Now there were Jews living in Jerusalem, devout men from every nation under heaven. And when the sound occurred, the crowd came together, and were bewildered because each one of them was hearing them speak in his own language."

This made me wonder, "Did the apostles then remember what Jesus had said to them only days before: "But you will receive power when the Holy Spirit has come upon you; and you shall be My witnesses both in Jerusalem, and in all Judea and Samaria, and even to the remotest part of the earth."

In verses 7 and 8, Dr. Luke records what I like to call "Phase 1: Jerusalem." And, how did those in Jerusalem respond to this strange phenomenon? Luke tells us, "They were amazed and astonished, saying, 'Why, are not these who are speaking Galileans? And how is it that we each hear them in our own language to which we were born?'" Now, certainly they must have been awe-struck that these mostly Galilean fishermen could speak in their native languages.

I find it interesting that the good doctor did not write anything about what the apostles were first saying to these Jews from all over the world. But, in verses 9-11, he lists the countries where they were all from and then adds, these were "both Jews and proselytes," that is, Gentile converts to Judaism."

As the apostles continued to speak in the native languages of those Jews who had gathered to celebrate Pentecost, Luke wrote in verses 12 and 13, "And they all continued in amazement and great perplexity, saying to one another, 'What does this mean?' But others were mocking and saying, 'They are full of sweet wine.'" In other words, some in the crowd thought the apostles had a little too much to drink! Now, what happens next is truly amazing. So, put down the remote and listen up!

In verse 14, Luke tells us that Peter got up and took his stand with the eleven. Talk about unity. Keep in mind, someone had just accused them of being drunk! Here's what Peter said: "Men of Judea and all you who live in

Jerusalem, let this be known to you and give heed to my words, 'For these men are not drunk, as you suppose, for it is only the third hour of the day (9 a.m.); but this is what was spoken of through the prophet Joel." Get this, Peter begins to preach from Joel 2:28-32 where the Lord God says:

"And it shall be in the last days (he's now got my attention), that I will pour out My Spirit on all mankind; and your sons and your daughters shall prophesy, and your young men shall see visions, and your old men shall dream dreams; even on my bond slaves, both men and women, I will in those days pour forth of My Spirit and they shall prophesy. And I will grant wonders in the sky above and signs on the earth below, blood and fire, and vapor of smoke. The sun will be turned into darkness and the moon into blood, before the great and glorious Day of the Lord shall come. And it shall be that everyone who calls on the Name of the Lord will be saved.'"

Wow! Wow! Wow! What a first message! Peter, the self-righteous and prideful former fisherman-turned preacher tells this large, Jewish crowd (which could have been upwards of a million people) about "the last days" (that is, of Israel's history) which will include: prophecy, visions, dreams, a pouring out of the Holy Spirit, wonders in the sky, signs on the earth, blood, fire, smoke, the sun turning into darkness, the moon into blood "before the great and glorious Day of the Lord." Note: This prophecy was one with a "double fulfillment" which was partially fulfilled on the day of Pentecost in Jerusalem and will be totally fulfilled during the so-called "Tribulation," leading up to the return of the Lord Jesus Christ to set up His kingdom on the earth!

Next, Peter concludes this portion of his message, saying, "And it shall be that everyone who calls on the name of the Lord will be saved!" Note: Paul uses this same verse in Romans 10:13. I like what William MacDonald says about "calling on the name of the Lord" in his Believer's Bible Commentary: "The name of the Lord is an expression that includes all that the Lord is. Thus, to call on His name is to call on Himself as the true object of faith and as the only way of salvation." Amen to that!

In the previous verse, Peter had boldly told the crowd about "calling on the name of the Lord." Then, in verse 22, he begins to tell them exactly Who this Lord is, saying He is: "Jesus the Nazarene, a man attested to you by God Who gave testimony with miracles and wonders and signs which God performed through Him in your midst, just as you yourselves know." Earlier on at the beginning of Jesus's ministry, the Jewish leader, Nicodemus, in John 3:2, recognized something special about Jesus. Saying, "Rabbi, we know that You have come from God as a teacher; for no one can do these signs that You do unless God is with him." Later, we know from John 7:50 and 51 that Nicodemus, perhaps now a believer in Jesus, became a defender of Him before the Pharisees. Then, along with a fellow believer, Joseph of Arimathea, prepared the body of their Messiah and Savior for burial and laid Him in the tomb (John 19:38-42).

Peter, filled with the Holy Spirit, continued his message to the Jews, in verses 23 and 24, getting right to the point: "This Man (Jesus), delivered over by the predetermined plan and foreknowledge of God, you nailed to a cross by the hands of godless men and put Him to death." Wow! Talk about speaking the truth in boldness and love. He continued, "But God raised Him up again, putting an end to the agony of death, since it was impossible for Him to be held in its power." Another Wow! Peter had just presented them with the Gospel: the death, burial and resurrection of Jesus Christ which Paul would later write about in I Corinthians 15:1-4.

In verses 25-31, Peter quotes from Psalm 16:8-11 where David wrote of the resurrection of Christ and, from Psalm 132:11, of God's promise "to seat a descendant of David on His throne" which He did, as we read in the genealogies of Joseph in Matthew 1:6 and of Mary in Luke 3:31.

In verse 32, Peter said, "This Jesus God raised up again, to which we are all witnesses." Drum roll please! And, in grand style, he concludes, in verses 33-36, saying, "Therefore having been exalted to the right hand of God, and having received from the Father the promise of the Holy Spirit, He has poured forth this which you both see and hear. For it was not David who ascended into heaven, but he himself says: 'The Lord said to My Lord, sit at My right hand, until I make Your enemies a footstool for your feet.' Therefore, let all the house of Israel know for certain that God has made Him both Lord and Christ – this Jesus whom you crucified." Ouch!!

Now, you would think this large crowd of Jews would, at this point, want to stone Peter and the other apostles for accusing them of crucifying Jesus. But, by the grace, mercy and power of God, the opposite happened. Luke writes in verse 37: "Now when they heard this, they were pierced to the heart, and said to Peter and the rest of the apostles, 'Brethren, what shall we do?'" Wow! Wow! Wow! What shall we do! Wouldn't it be wonderful if that would be the response to all of our messages!

Peter then responds in verse 38, "Repent, and be baptized in the name of Jesus Christ for the forgiveness of your sins; and (as a bonus) you will receive the gift of the Holy Spirit."

So, let me pause here to tell you something about what it means to "repent." The Greek word is metanoeo which, according to William Vine, in his "Expository Dictionary of New Testament Words," means to "change one's mind or purpose, always in the New Testament, involving a change for the better." Question, "What were they to change their mind about?" Let me give you an example from today. There are many people in the world who believe they are "good people." Yet, the Word of God (Romans 3:23) says, "For all have sinned and fall short of the glory of God." Even back in the Old Testament, in Isaiah 53:6, we read, "All of us like sheep have gone astray, each of us has turned to his own way." Jesus Himself told the rich, young ruler, in Matthew 19:17, "Only God is good." In fact, He is holy, perfect and righteous. We are all unholy, imperfect and unrighteous and deserve to spend our eternity in hell.

Yet, if we change our minds about Who

God is (holy, perfect, righteous) and who we are (wretched, sinful and rebellious sinners who deserve to die and go to hell for eternity), but through faith in the shed blood of Jesus on the cross for our sins, His burial and resurrection from the dead, we can be declared "holy" by God and go to heaven when we die. Glory to God and Hallelujah!

Now, getting back to Acts 2:38, Peter said to the Jews, "Repent, and each of you be baptized in the name of Jesus Christ for the forgiveness of your sins; and you will receive the gift of the Holy Spirit." When you read this, it might sound like "works righteousness" which, sadly, is alive and being taught and believed in many so-called "Christian" churches today where the sacraments of baptism and communion, along with other "good works," are added to the grace of God for salvation. Let me make it clear: It is only by God's grace through faith in Christ alone and not our good works, that we are saved from our sins and have eternal life (Ephesians 2:8, 9).

Dr. Luke, in verse 40, gives us a better

take on this: "And with many other words he (Peter) solemnly testified and kept on exhorting them, saying, 'Be saved from this perverse generation!'" Next, in verse 41, the good doctor records something pretty amazing: "So, then, those who had received his words were baptized; and that day there were added three thousand souls." Did you get that? Peter preached Christ as the only Savior from sin and by the power of the Holy Spirit, 3,000 people got saved and were baptized.

That's the way it should be in all of our churches today: Christ is preached; sinners come under conviction they are lost, doomed to hell and need a Savior; then, believe in Jesus to be their Savior and out of obedience to Him, get baptized, which, according to William Vine, "identifies the believer with Christ's death, burial and resurrection." Note: Neither baptism nor communion nor confirmation nor church membership nor prayer nor giving money to the church nor doing anything else saves you from your sins. As I just said, Salvation is all by God's grace through faith in Christ and not by works (Ephesians 2:8, 9). Period! End of story! No "ifs, ands or buts!"

Oh, and one more comment about what happened on Pentecost: The church was born! With 3,000 new members it was a mega-church at that! And you thought that was something new to our generation. Wrong! What happened next was also truly amazing.

Dr. Luke records in verse 42: "They were continually devoting themselves to the apostles' teaching and to fellowship, to the breaking of bread and to prayer." Note: These were and should be today the four main characteristics or ministries of the church: the teaching (and preaching) of the Word of God, the sharing of a common life together, the celebration of the Lord's Supper (which early on included fellowship meals but were later discontinued because of gluttony and drunkenness) and prayer.

In verses 43-47, Luke tells us a little more of what this church looked like: "Everyone kept feeling a sense of awe; and many wonders and signs were taking place through the apostles. And all those who believed were together and had all things in common; and they began selling their possessions and were sharing them with all, as anyone might have need. Day by day continuing with one mind in the temple, and breaking bread from house to house, they were taking their meals together with gladness and sincerity of heart, praising God and having favor with all people. And the Lord added to their number day by day those who were being saved." Wow! Praise the Lord! Glory to God!

Oh, and one more note: the words "day by day" made me think of the play, "Godspell" which I auditioned for in Boston about 50 years ago and am still waiting to hear if I got a part or not (I am thinking not!).

Act 3

Dr. Luke, in verses 1-10, tells us an amazing story of Peter and John going up to the temple at 3:00 pm for prayer when a man who had been lame from birth was brought in and set down at the gate of the temple called "Beautiful" to beg for alms. The temple itself was beautiful after it had been restored by King Herod. You might remember this from Mark 13:1, when the apostles were admiring the "wonderful stones and buildings" of the temple.

Now, back to Peter and John. As they were going into the temple, the lame man, as was his custom, asked the two apostles for alms (money). And, much to his surprise I am sure, Luke tells us in verse 4, "But Peter, along with John, fixed his gaze on him and said, 'Look at us!'" And, in verse 5, Luke records, "And he began to give them his attention, expecting to receive something from them."

What happens next is truly miraculous. Oops, I'm getting a little ahead of myself. Sorry about that. Drum roll, please! We read, "But

Peter said, 'I do not possess silver and gold, but what I do have I give to you (goosebumps): In the name of Jesus Christ the Nazarene – walk.'"

Now, I don't know about you, but if I was the man, I am probably thinking, "yeah, right!" Peter didn't waste any time, as the good doctor records, in verses 7 and 8, "And, seizing him by the right hand, he raised him up; and immediately his feet and ankles were strengthened. With a leap he stood upright and began to walk (more goosebumps); and he entered the temple with them, walking and leaping and praising God." As someone once told me, "He asked for alms and he got legs!" I know that was "lame!" As my mother would say rather sarcastically when I told her a joke, "Ha, ha, very funny!"

Then, we get to verses 9 and 10 which will play a part in another story down the road, but first things first, as Luke writes, "And all the people saw him walking and praising God; and they were taking note of him as being the one who used to sit at the Beautiful Gate of the temple to beg alms, and they were filled with wonder and amazement at what had happened to him."

In verses 11-12, The good doctor tells us that "While he (the lame man who was healed) was clinging to Peter and John (hard for me to picture that with both men), all the people ran together to them at the so-called portico (or porch) of Solomon, full of amazement." When Peter saw the crowd following them, he said to the crowd, "Men of Israel, why are you amazed at this, or why do you gaze at us, as if by our own power or piety we had made him walk."

Peter then launches into his second sermon which you can read in verses 13-26, but let me give you some of the highlights from verses 13-15 where Peter said: "The God of Abraham, Isaac and Jacob, the God of our fathers, has glorified His servant Jesus, the one whom you delivered and disowned in the presence of Pilate, when he had decided to release Him. But you disowned the Holy and Righteous One and asked for a murderer (Barabbas) to be granted to you, but put to death the Prince of life, the one whom God raised from the dead, a fact to which we are witnesses. And on the basis of faith in His name, it is the name of Jesus which has strengthened this man whom you see and know; and the faith which comes through Him has given him this perfect health in the presence of you all (Luke must have been from the south)."

Peter then very graciously says, in verses 17-21, "And now, brethren, I know that you acted in ignorance, just as your rulers did also. But the things which God announced beforehand by the mouth of all the prophets, that His Christ would suffer, He has thus fulfilled. Therefore, repent and return, so that your sins may be wiped away, in order that times of refreshing may come from the presence of the Lord; and that He may send Jesus, the Christ appointed for you whom heaven must receive (His ascension) until the period of restoration of all things (Christ's second coming) about which God spoke by the mouth of His prophets from ancient time."

Note: Here, Peter was not only referring to the gospel (the death, burial and resurrection of Jesus), but also to His ascension and second coming to the earth which, as a Jew, you can read about in Zechariah 14 and Ezekiel 40-48 and, as a Gentile, in Revelation 19:1-6 which is also known as the "Millennial Kingdom."

Act 4

And, just when it looked like things were going smoothly for the new church, Satan stirred up "the priests, the captain of the temple guard and the Sadducees against Peter and John because they were "proclaiming in Jesus the resurrection of the dead" (which the Sadducees did not believe). So, we read, in verse 3, that the Jewish leaders arrested Peter and John and put them in jail. However, the good doctor/statistician reported: "But many of those who had heard the message believed; and the number of the men came to be about five thousand." Glory to God!

Meanwhile, back at the Sanhedrin (the religious court of Judaism which was made up of 70 elders plus the High Priest), they gathered to discuss what to do with Peter and John. Interestingly enough, they were not as interested in their preaching as they were in their healing of the lame man from the previous chapter. Not only was the High Priest, Caiaphas, there, but also the previous High Priest, Annas, and two other men, John and

Alexander, whom Luke tells us "were of the high priestly family." Note: We know from the Gospel of John (18:12-27) that Jesus appeared before Annas and Caiaphas before He was brought before Pilate who, to keep the Jews from rioting, ordered Jesus' to be crucified in fulfillment of Isaiah 53. Now, it was Peter and John's turn before the Sanhedrin, thus fulfilling what Jesus said to His disciples in Mark 13:9 and 11: "Be on your guard; for they (the Sanhedrin) will deliver you to the courts, and you will be flogged in the synagogues … "When they arrest you and hand you over, do not worry beforehand about what you are to say, but say whatever is given you in that hour; for it is not you who speak, but it is the Holy Spirit" (which had been recently given them on Pentecost). Isn't that just like God! So, let the trial begin!

The prosecution begins its case in verse 7, with a question for Peter and John, "By what power, or in what name, have you done this (that is, healed the lame man)?" Luke then records the defense: "Then Peter, filled with the Holy Spirit, said to them, 'Rulers and elders of the people, if we are on trial today for a benefit done to a sick man, as to how this man has been made well, let it be known to all of you and to all the people of Israel, that by the name of Jesus Christ the Nazarene, whom you crucified (bold!), whom God raised from the dead (take that, Sadducees) – by this name this man stands here before you in good health."

If that wasn't bold enough, Peter said, "He (Jesus) is the Stone which was rejected by you, the builders, but which became the Chief Corner Stone (in fulfillment of Psalm 118:22). Wow! Then Peter boldly proclaimed, "And there is salvation in no one else; for there is no other name under heaven that has been given among men by which we must be saved." Wow! Wow! Wow! Glory to God! Hallelujah! Thank You, Jesus! Thank You, Holy Spirit!

Keep in mind, this is the same Peter who, in the flesh, denied his Lord three times in John 18:15-18, 25-27 to save his own skin. Now, filled with the Holy Spirit, Peter and, I am sure, John, were willing to proclaim and die for Jesus, their Messiah and Savior!

I like what the good doctor then records in verse 13: "Now as they observed the confidence of Peter and John and understood that they were uneducated and untrained men (except for fishing), they were amazed, and began to recognize them as having been with Jesus." So, let me ask you and me a question: "Would there be enough evidence of my (our) witness that others would know we had been with Jesus?"

In verse 14, Dr. Luke adds the prosecution's response: "And seeing the man who had been healed standing with them, they had nothing to say in reply." I love it! Note: I am sure they all probably had seen this man for many, many years, begging for alms at the gate of the temple. Maybe, they had even thrown a coin or two his way. They knew he was lame from birth. Now, miraculously, he is able to walk, run and jump for joy because of Jesus! This certainly put a damper on their prosecution.

Amazingly, Dr. Luke is privy to the Council's discussion about this dilemma, recording them saying, in verses 16 and 17, "What shall we do with these men? For the fact that a noteworthy miracle has taken place through them (Peter and John) is apparent to all who live in Jerusalem, and we cannot deny it. But so that it will not spread any further among the people (yeah, right; good luck with that one!), let us warn them to speak no longer to any man in this name." Note: We should never be ashamed to speak the Name of Jesus, the Son of God and our Savior.

In the next verse (18), Luke records: "And when they had summoned them, they commanded them not to speak or teach at all in the name of Jesus." So, how did that go?

Well, all we have to do is read verses 19 and 20 to find out. Luke records: "But Peter and John answered and said to them, 'Whether it is right in the sight of God to give heed to you rather than to God, you be the judge; for we cannot stop speaking about what we have seen and heard." Another wow! What a powerful witness for Jesus!

Luke then tells us, in verses 21 and 22,

"When they had threatened them further, they let them go (finding no basis on which to punish them) on account of the people, because they were all glorifying God for what had happened; for the man was more than forty years old on whom this miracle had been performed."

Next, Dr. Luke joyfully records, in verse 23, "When they had been released, they went to their own companions and reported all that the chief priests and the elders had said to them." Their brothers and sisters in Christ responded, in verses 24-26, "by lifting their voices with one accord and saying, 'O Lord, it is You who made the heaven and earth and the sea, and all that is in them, who by the Holy Spirit, through the mouth of our father David Your servant said, in Psalm 2:1, 2, 'Why did the Gentiles rage and the peoples devise futile things? The kings of the earth took their stand, and the rulers were gathered together against the Lord and against His Christ.'"

Sadly, ever since Satan and his angels rebelled against the triune God (Father, Son and Holy Spirit), they have seduced many a Jew and Gentile to follow their rebellion against the Godhead. So, we are not surprised to hear Jesus say, in Matthew 7:13, 14: "For the gate is wide and the way is broad that leads to destruction, and there are many who enter it. For the gate is small and the way is narrow that leads to life, and there are few who find it." Note: I am so thankful to God that He has shown me the narrow way to life through faith in Christ. How about you? Please know that no matter how messed up your life has been, God can and will forgive all your sins and give you eternal life by putting your faith in Jesus, His death, burial and resurrection.

Next, in Acts 4:29, 30, the good doctor records the church praying with a slight imprecation, "And now, Lord, take note of their threats." Prayers of Imprecation were often prayed in the Psalms (7, 35, 55, 58, 59, 69, 79, 109, 137, 139, 140) where the people of Israel were asking God to get their enemies and get them good.

Keep in mind, the Book of Acts is a book of transition from Israel to the Church, and things will be different. In fact, Jesus gave us a glimpse of this in His "Sermon on the Mount" (which, get this, according to a survey I once read, some people actually think Jesus preached on horseback) when He said, in Matthew 5:43, 44, "You have heard that it was said, 'You shall love your neighbor and hate your enemy' (Leviticus 19:18; Deuteronomy 23:3-6). But I say to you, love your enemies and pray for those who persecute you."

On a brighter note, the church also prayed, "and grant that Your bond-servants may speak Your word with all confidence (boldness, KJV), while You extend Your hand to heal, and signs and wonders take place through the name of Your holy servant Jesus." Note: As we continue on in Acts, we will see a lot of praying by God's people. Someone once told me, "God answers prayers in one of three ways: 'Yes, No and Wait!'" And, from my own experience, I would add a fourth: "Silence!" You can see that in the Book of Job who, as I said in my first book, "When Thorns Remain," along with Paul, are two of my heroes of the faith because of the suffering they endured to the glory of God.

Dr. Luke then adds something rather dramatic in verse 31: "And when they had prayed, the place where they had gathered together was shaken, and they were all filled with the Holy Spirit and began to speak the word of God with boldness." May we pray for the Lord to give us more boldness as we share Christ in our preaching, teaching and living to the glory of God. Recently, He has given me the opportunity to do this through my blog at dougsdailydoings for which I am most thankful.

Back in Acts 2:42, Dr. Luke pointed out the four-fold purpose of the church: The "teaching of the Word of God (and let me add as "the whole truth and nothing but the truth"), fellowship (sharing life together), breaking of bread (celebrating the Lord's Supper) and prayer."

Years ago, a pastor friend told me someone in his congregation said to him, "I'm sick and tired of you preaching about us being an Acts 2:42 church!" Really? Unless he was preaching that and only that every Sunday, I don't know about you, but I believe there is nothing wrong with being reminded of what God's Word says about what our main focus as a church should be.

In verses 32-37, we get our first glimpse of what "sharing life together" meant. Dr. Luke records: "And the congregation of those who believed were of one heart and soul; and not one of them claimed that anything belonging to him was his own, but all things were common property to them." Wow! How cool was that!

Then, in verse 33, we read, "And with <u>great</u> power the apostles were giving testimony to the resurrection of the Lord Jesus, and abundant (<u>great, KJV</u>) grace was upon them all." Remember, Jesus had appeared to the apostles on a number of occasions after His crucifixion and before His ascension to the throne of God in heaven. I just love the words, "and abundant (<u>great</u>) grace was upon them all." Maybe you read this in a previous book, but "grace" is my favorite word and especially in

Paul's writings where he uses the word "grace" 83 times in his 13 letters (and 8 more times if you believe he wrote Hebrews). Oh, and one more item of "trivia," Luke uses the word "great" (megas in the Greek) 17 times in his gospel and 23 times in Acts.

Next, we read, in verses 34 and 35, something pretty amazing: "For there was not a needy person among them, for all who were owners of land or houses would sell them and bring the proceeds of the sales and lay them at the apostles' feet, and they would be distributed to each as any had need." Wow! Wow! Wow! This was not like Robin Hood who, along with his merry men, would "steal from the rich and give to the poor." This was much different because there was no stealing at all. It was simply men and women who, under the leading of the Holy Spirit, recognized that everything they had belonged to God. When they saw a need in the church, they responded accordingly. As a result, all the needs were met! Praise the Lord! This is a good reminder to all of us in the church today that we are to be good stewards of the money and possessions God has blessed us with, especially in regards to the needs of our local church.

Back in my previous book, "Laughing with Luke," I mentioned that Luke was my favorite gospel because, more than any other of the gospel writers, he tells us about real people whose names we often take for granted, but each with a story to tell. So, true to form, Luke tells us about a man by the name of "Joseph" whom he describes as a "Levite of Cyprian birth" which means he was a Jewish priest from Cyprus who had probably come to Jerusalem to celebrate Pentecost. He must have listened to Peter's message, got saved and, we are told, "owned a piece of land, sold it and brought the money and laid it at the apostles feet" which was both amazing and unusual since, as a Levite, the Lord, and not land, was to be his portion. Interestingly enough, the good doctor tells us this Joseph of Cyprus was given a nickname by the apostles: "Barnabas which means Son of Encouragement." Note: Most believers probably don't know that Jesus gave out nicknames as well, as we read, in Mark 3: 16, 17, "And He (Jesus) appointed the twelve:

Simon (to whom He gave the name Peter), and James the son of Zebedee, and John the brother of James (to them He gave the name Boanerges, which means, 'Sons of Thunder.'" Note: A friend of mine from the local Police Department has come up with some unusual nicknames for me which I like: The Dooginator; Doogasaurus Rex; Deputy Doug!

Act 5

At the end of Act 4, Dr. Luke told us about an extraordinary gift of money Barnabas had given to the church from some land he had sold to the glory of God. Now, in Act 5, Luke is going to tell us about a couple who also gave a "gift" to the church which, as we shall see, was not to the glory of God and resulted in the judgment of God.

The couple's names were Ananias and Sapphira. They also owned some property which they sold and gave some of the profit to the church and kept some of it for themselves which, on the surface seemed okay. But they gave the impression they had given all of the money to the church when, in fact, they had given some and kept some for themselves.

Then, we read in verses 3 and 4, "But Peter said, 'Ananias, why has Satan filled your heart to lie to the Holy Spirit and to keep back some of the price of the land? While it remained unsold, did it not remain your own? And after it was sold, was it not under your control? Why is it that you have conceived this deed in your heart? You have not lied to men but to God.'"

What happens next is right out of the Old Testament where the Lord would often judge sin right on the spot. Dr Luke records, in verse 5, "And as he (Ananias) heard these words, Ananias fell down and breathed his last." Wow! Luke then adds, "and great fear came over all who heard of it!" Ah, yeah!

Next, in verse 6, we read, "The young men (Matt and Mike by us) got up and covered him up, and after carrying him out, they buried him." Now, you would think Sapphira would have been grieving her husband's death. Well, according to what we read in verse 7, about three hours later, she appeared and didn't even know her husband had died. Peter asked her about the price she and Ananias had gotten for the land. She agreed that was the price. Then, in verse 9, Luke records: "Why is it that you have agreed together to put the Spirit of the Lord to the test? Behold, the feet of those who have buried your husband are at the door, and they will carry you out as well."

In verse 10, Luke reports, "And immediately she fell at his feet and breathed her last, and the young men came in and found her dead, and they carried her out and buried her beside her husband." As you can imagine, we should not be surprised to read in the next verse (11), "And great fear came over the whole church, and over all who heard of these things." Note: Sometimes, I wonder, "What would God have to do today to bring "great fear over the whole church?" Then again, maybe I don't want to know.

Oh, on an embarrassing note: I can remember a time when I was young in the ministry and can't remember what I was preaching about, but I was so sure of what I was saying that I made the following statement: "And, if I am wrong, may God strike me dead in the pulpit!" Wow! How dumb was that! I guess I can be thankful we are now in the age of grace or else I might have had the Shimon boys carrying me out as well!

In the next 5 verses (12-16), the good

doctor records how the Spirit of the Lord was moving in the early church and throughout Jerusalem with "signs, wonders" and, more importantly, many people coming to faith in Jesus as their Savior and Lord.

Note: Once one becomes a believer in Jesus, you soon realize that, when the Lord is doing a mighty work through you, Satan is waiting in the wings to undo it and you. That's exactly what we see in verses 17 and 18 where we read, "But the high priest rose up, along with all his associates (the Sadducees), and they were filled with jealousy. They laid hands on the apostles and put them in the public jail." Another note: The Lord knows the devil's every move and counters him, in verse 19, by sending one of His angels during the night to open the gates of the prison for the apostles to escape and to "speak to the people in the temple the whole message of this Life," a reference to Jesus, "the Way, The Truth and the Life (John 14:6)."

So, at daybreak, the apostles go right back to the temple and begin to teach the people about Jesus, the Messiah and Savior. Meanwhile, back at the Sanhedrin, they sent orders to the prison for the apostles to be released and brought before the Council. What happens next is kind of funny: the officers go to the prison to get the apostles and find they are not there. They go back to the Council and say to them: "We found the prison house locked quite securely and the guards standing at the doors; but when we opened them, we found no one inside!"

Next, we read, in verse 24: "Now when the captain of the temple guard and the chief priests heard these words, they were greatly perplexed about them as to what would come of this. Note: We know from several accounts that, if the prison guards let their prisoners escape, they would face the death penalty. One of those accounts was in Matthew 28:11-15 where the guards who kept watch over the tomb where Jesus' body lay, faced the death penalty for "sleeping on the job" and letting Jesus escape, only to be bribed by the Council to say that "His disciples came by night and stole Him away while we were asleep."

Personally, I don't see how anyone could have believed that Jesus' cowardly disciples could have overpowered the Roman guards and taken His body. But, they did and, Matthew records in verse 15: "and this story was widely spread among the Jews, and is to this day."

What happens next is kind of funny. Luke records, in verse 25, "But someone came and reported to them (the Council), 'The men whom you put in prison are standing in the temple and teaching the people!'" Peter and the other apostles weren't going to let these religious leaders get in their way from telling others about Jesus. Now they had public opinion on their side, as we read in the next verse, "Then the captain went along with the officers and proceeded to bring them back without violence (for they were afraid of the people, that they might be stoned)."

In verses 27 and 28, Luke tells us that the soldiers then brought the apostles before the Council where the high priest addressed them, saying, "We gave you strict orders not to continue teaching in 'this name' (notice he wouldn't even say the name "Jesus"). He continued, "and yet, you have filled Jerusalem with your teaching and intend to bring this man's blood upon us." How ironic, as Matthew records in his gospel (27:24, 25) of Pilate saying, "I am innocent of this Man's blood and all the people said, 'His blood shall be on us and our children!'" Sadly, it was in 70 A.D. when about a million Jews were killed and their temple was destroyed by the Romans.

I just love Peter's and the other apostles' response to the high priest, "We must obey God rather than men." Amen and Amen! Then, they continued, "The God of our fathers (notice their use of the word "our" because they were just as Jewish as their leaders) raised up Jesus, whom you put to death by hanging Him on a cross. He is the one whom God exalted to His right hand as a Prince and Savior, to grant repentance to Israel, and forgiveness of sins. And we are witnesses of these things; and so is the Holy Spirit, whom God has given to those who obey Him." Wow! Bravo! But did the Jews even hear what they said? You betcha! They were under conviction, but instead of agreeing with the apostles that they were sinners who needed a Savior, they "intended to kill them."

Not all of them. Once again, the good doctor introduces us to another real human being, "a Pharisee named Gamaliel, a teacher of the Law and respected by all the people." And, I might add, a teacher of one Saul of Tarsus (Acts 22:3) whom we, as believers in Jesus, would come to know and love as the apostle Paul.

While the other members of the Council wanted to kill the apostles, Gamaliel took a more measured response to the proceedings. First, in verse 34, Luke tells us that he "gave orders to put the men outside for a short time." Then, in verses 35-37, he began to give the Council some examples of other men who "rose up" as Messiahs, like Theudas who had a following of 400 men, but was killed and all who followed him were dispersed and came to nothing." Next, he told the Council about "Judas of Galilee who, drew away some people after him; he too perished, and all those who followed him were scattered." Then, Gamaliel gave this advice: "So in the present case, I say to you, stay away from these men and let them alone, for if this plan or action is of men, it will be overthrown; but if it is of God, you will not be able to overthrow them; or else you may even be found fighting against God."

Luke then records in verse 40: "They took his advice, and after calling the apostles in, they flogged them and ordered them not to speak in the name of Jesus, and then released them." I just love how the apostles responded. Luke records in verse 41, "So they went on their way from the presence of the Council, rejoicing that they had been considered worthy to suffer shame for His name." Wow! They rejoiced because they had "suffered shame for His (Jesus) name." Glory to God! Comment: We should be willing to do the same.

This previous account is very personal to me. When I was in seminary, I met a woman who was part of a Christian theater group and on occasion, would fall asleep and get this, "dream out loud" in a conversation with the Lord Jesus. In one of her dreams, I heard her say the Lord told her she would experience a "virgin birth" like Mary's and that the two of us would get married. When I told one of the guys in my dorm about this, he thought it was "pretty cool" and that I should tell others about these experiences. I wasn't so sure. So, I decided to see my Psychology Professor and ask him what he thought about this.

He listened; then I believe, led by the Holy Spirit, brought up the account of Gamaliel which I had never heard of before. Like Gamaliel's advice to the Council, my professor told me, "If these things are of God, they would come true. If not, they would simply go away." I took his advice and gave it some time. After a while, I could see these things were not of God, but of the devil, and broke off the relationship. Thank You, Jesus, for protecting me!

Now, back to Luke 5, verse 42 where, after the apostles had been flogged and told not to speak again about Jesus, Luke records: "And every day, in the temple and from house to house, they kept right on teaching and preaching Jesus as the Christ." Wow! Wow!

Wow! The flogging didn't stop them; the orders to stop preaching about Jesus didn't stop them. What courage! So, they continued witnessing of Jesus as the Christ. Did you notice where they were witnessing? Right "in the temple" where the Council could see them, as well as "from house to house" where the common people could hear about Jesus. Remember back in Matthew 10, the Lord had given the apostles instructions about who to witness to and not to witness to. By the way, that is still a good model for us today.

Act 6

In Acts 6, Luke tells us about a problem in the church which didn't surprise me with the 5,000 or so members. Actually, I'm sure you also know there can be problems in smaller churches as I well-know, having served in three of them. Satan doesn't discriminate and will try to stir things up one way or another to keep the church from being the church. I'm sure you can all relate.

Dr. Luke records in verse 1: "Now at the time while the disciples were increasing (praise God!), a complaint (murmuring, KJV) arose on the part of the Hellenistic (Greek-speaking Jews) against the native Hebrews, because their widows were being overlooked in the daily serving of food." Now, keep in mind, the church had grown to "about five thousand men" (Acts 4:4) plus women and children. That's a lot of mouths to feed. For some unknown reason, the Jewish widows were being fed and the Greek widows weren't. So, what did the apostles do? Luke tells us in verse 2, they called a meeting and told the members about the need! Then, in verses 3 and 4, they told the church family what they needed to do, saying, "It is not desirable for us to neglect the word of God in order to serve tables. Therefore, brethren, select from among you seven men of good reputation, full of the Spirit and of wisdom, whom we may put in charge of this task. But we will devote ourselves to prayer and to the ministry of the word." That was brilliant!

Now, I can't even imagine how they were going to pick out seven men out of 5,000 for this ministry, unless the Holy Spirit had something to do with it which He did, as we see in verse 5 where Luke records: "The statement found approval with the <u>whole</u> congregation." Did you get that? The whole congregation of 5,000+ approved the apostles' idea! Glory to God!

Then, Luke continues, "And they chose Stephen, a man full of faith and the Holy Spirit, and Philip, Prochorus, Nicanor, Timon, Parmenas and Nicolas, a proselyte (that is, a Gentile convert to Judaism) from Antioch."

Next, Luke records in verse 6: "And

these they brought before the apostles; and after praying, they laid their hands on them." Charles Ryrie comments: "The laying on of hands was a formal sign of appointment to this service." The result: The Greek- speaking widows were taken care of with what we would call the first "deacons" in the church. Take that, Satan! As we shall see, he'd be back soon enough.

In verse 7, the good doctor adds: "The word of God kept spreading; and the number of disciples continued to increase greatly in Jerusalem, and a great many of the (Jewish) priests were becoming obedient to the faith." Wow! Did you hear that – "a great many of the priests were becoming obedient to the faith!" Glory to God! Hallelujah! That should be an inspiration for us, including me, to pray for the salvation of those unsaved pastors and priests in our communities.

In verse 8, Dr. Luke begins to tell us about Stephen who was one of the seven deacons we learned about in verse 5. I probably told you this in my last book, but Luke tells us more about real people than any other of the gospel writers and I just love that. In verse 8, Luke writes: "And Stephen, full of grace and power, was performing great wonders and signs among the people." Not surprisingly, Satan took note of that and began an all-out assault against Stephen. In verse 9, Luke records: "But some men from what was called the Synagogue of the Freedmen, including both Cyrenians and Alexandrians, and some from Cilicia and Asia, rose up and argued with Stephen." Charles Ryrie comments: "These were Jewish freedmen, or descendants of men freed from slavery, from the various places mentioned in the verse. They had their own synagogue in Jerusalem." The apostle John, in Revelation 2:9, called places like this "a synagogue of Satan!"

I just love what Luke says about their attack in verse 10: "But they were unable to cope with (resist, KJV) the wisdom and the Spirit with which he (Stephen) was speaking." Glory to God! Take that, Satan!

Well, as you probably guessed, Satan wasn't too pleased with the results of his first attack. So, he then launched a second volley which Luke records in verse 11, "by secretly inducing men to say, 'We have heard him say blasphemous words against Moses and against God.'" Sounds a lot like Jesus' accusers before Caiaphas the high priest in Matthew 26:57-68.

Luke then tells us in verses 12-14, that his (Stephen's) enemies "stirred up the people, the elders and the scribes, and they came up to him and dragged him away and brought him to the Council. They put forward false witnesses who said, 'this man incessantly speaks against this holy place (the temple) and the Law; for we have heard him say that this Nazarene, Jesus, will destroy this place and alter the customs which Moses handed down to us.'" The next verse (15) is priceless: "And fixing their gaze on him, all who were sitting in the Council saw his face like the face of an angel." Wow! What a testimony without even saying a word in his defense! Glory to God! But, did that change anything with his accusers? Let's find out in the next chapter.

Act 7

In Act 7, Stephen gives a defense to the Freedmen and the Council. I just love how he responds to their accusations. Luke records: "Hear me, brethren and fathers!" Wow! He could have very easily called them a bunch of devil worshipers and idiots; but he didn't. This made me think of what Paul said in Colossians 4:6, "Let your speech always be with grace, as though seasoned with salt, so that you will know how you should respond to each person."

Stephen began his defense with a history lesson, recalling for them (the Jews) how God had called Abraham to leave his home country of Chaldea (Babylon) to go to Haran and, after his father had died, to Palestine (Israel). Then, he gave a rather complete account of the patriarchs (Abraham, Isaac and Jacob) and how Joseph rescued and provided for his family in a time of famine. Then he went on to remind them of Moses and the "burning bush" and how the Lord God appeared and spoke to him, telling him that he would lead his people out of slavery and on to the Promised Land over a period of 40 years which included a time when Aaron would lead the people into making a golden calf to worship while Moses was up on Mt. Sinai getting the Ten Commandments from the Lord. Steven continued his defense by reminding the Jews about King David's desire to build a temple for the Lord which his son, Solomon, was able to do. He then quoted from Isaiah 61:1 and 2 reminding them, as William MacDonald wrote, "that buildings are not what really count with God but rather the moral and spiritual condition of men's lives. He looks for a broken and contrite heart, for a man who trembles at His word."

Then, in verses 51-53, Stephen boldly said to his enemies, "You men who are stiff-necked and uncircumcised in heart and ears are always resisting the Holy Spirit; you are doing just as your fathers did. Which one of the prophets did your fathers persecute? They killed those who had previously announced the coming of the Righteous One, whose betrayers and murderers you have now become; you who received the law as ordained by angels, and yet did not keep it." Pow! Right to the heart!

Another glory to God!

Now as you can imagine, the Council did not take very kindly to these words. In fact, Dr. Luke records in verse 54: "Now when they heard this (the Truth), they were cut to the quick, and they began gnashing their teeth at him. Then, in verses 55 and 56, we read: "But being full of the Holy Spirit, he gazed intently into heaven and saw the glory of God (goosebumps), and Jesus standing at the right hand of God (more goosebumps); and he said, 'Behold, I see the heavens opened up and the Son of Man standing at the right hand of God.'" Wow! Wow! Wow! Stephen got a "standing ovation" from Jesus, just before his death and going to be with His Savior and Lord!!!

In verses 57 and 58, Luke records: "But they (the Council) cried out with a loud voice, and covered their ears and rushed at him with one impulse. When they had driven him out of the city, they began stoning him; and the witnesses laid aside their robes at the feet of a young man named Saul."

As they continued to stone Stephen, what happened next, is truly amazing, inspirational and Christlike (more goosebumps). Luke writes: "Stephen called on the Lord and said, 'Lord Jesus, receive my spirit!' Then falling on his knees, he cried out with a loud voice, 'Lord, do not hold this sin against them.' Having said this, he fell asleep." Talk about being like Jesus in life and in death. Leave it to Luke to record, in his gospel (23:34), Jesus saying on the cross, "Father, forgive them; for they do not know what they are doing" and, in verse 46, "Jesus cried out with a loud voice and said, 'Father, into your hands I commit My spirit.' Having said this, he breathed His last."

Act 8

Talk about a tough "act" (did you get it?) to follow! Luke picks up the story with more of Saul's hatred of Jesus and His followers, as we read in Chapter 8:1, "Saul was in hearty agreement with putting him (Stephen) to death. And on that day a great persecution began against the church in Jerusalem, and they were all scattered throughout the regions of Judea and Samaria, except the apostles." I remember one of our missionaries, Rob Larkin, saying, "Acts 1:8 was fulfilled in Acts 8:1!" What did the Lord Jesus say to His apostles, in 1:8?" He said, "You will receive power when the Holy Spirit has come upon you; and you shall be my witnesses both in Jerusalem, and in all Judea and Samaria, and even to the remotest parts of the earth."

Then, in verse 2, Luke simply adds: "Some devout men buried Stephen, and made loud lamentation over him." Can you see why Luke is my favorite gospel writer? Without missing a beat, he writes in verse 3: "But Saul began ravaging the church, entering house after house, and dragging off men and women, he would put them in prison." Later on, in Galatians 1:13, in one of Paul's testimonies, he told the believers in Galatia, "For you heard of my former manner of life in Judaism, how I used to persecute the church of God beyond measure and tried to destroy it." Note: Just when you think your unsaved loved ones are too far gone for salvation, remember Saul who, by the grace of God, became Paul and went from being one of Satan's best disciples to one of Jesus' best to the glory of God. So, keep loving those unsaved loved ones and praying for them. You just never know what God is going to do.

Dr. Luke then records in verse 4: "Therefore, those who had been scattered went about preaching the word." Praise God! In verse 6, we learn that Philip, one of the original seven deacons in the church in Jerusalem (Acts 6:5), "went down to the city of Samaria and began proclaiming Christ to them." Charles Ryrie, in his Study Bible, comments on the Samaritans: "They were descendants of colonists whom the Assyrian kings planted in

Palestine after the fall of the Northern Kingdom in 722 BC. They were despised by the Jews because of their mixed Gentile blood and their different worship, which took place on Mt. Gerizim" (and not on Mount Zion/Jerusalem).

Note: Interestingly enough and just like God, He sent Philip, a Greek and a Gentile to go to the "half-Gentile" Samaritans to preach Christ to them (verse 5). The results were amazing, as we read in verses 6 and 7: "The crowds with one accord were giving attention to what was said by Philip, as they heard and saw signs which he was performing. For in the case of many who had unclean spirits, they were coming out of them shouting with a loud voice; and many who had been paralyzed and lame were healed." Glory to God! Then, Luke adds in verse 8: "So there was much rejoicing in that city." How exciting because now many of the Samaritans were coming to faith in Christ!

In verses 9 and 10, the good doctor introduces us to a magician by the name of Simon (not to be confused with Simon Peter) "who formerly was practicing magic in the city and astonishing the people of Samaria, claiming to be someone great; and they all, from the smallest to greatest, were giving attention to him, saying, 'This man is what is called the Great Power of God.'" Wow! How sad.

Now, wait a minute, Luke just told us this Simon was "formerly practicing magic in the city and astonishing the people of Samaria" to the point of being called "the Great Power of God." So, I would ask, "What happened to his 'magic and great power?'" I could be wrong, but I think we'll get a clue as we read "the rest of the story," as Paul Harvey would say.

When we read verse 11, it sounds like Simon was still pretty popular with the people of Samaria until we read, in verse 12, "But when they believed Philip preaching the good news about the kingdom of God and the name of Jesus Christ, they were being baptized, men and women alike." Now, all of a sudden, Simon wasn't so popular in Samaria.

In verse 13, we see the old expression, "If you can't beat em, join em." Luke writes, "Even Simon himself believed; and after being baptized, he continued on with Philip, and as he observed signs and great miracles taking place, he was constantly amazed." This old magician saw a new kind of power not based on deceit, but on something that Philip had and, as we shall see, he wanted.

In verses 14-16, Luke records: "Now when the apostles in Jerusalem heard that Samaria had received the word of God, they sent them Peter and John, who came down and prayed for them that they might receive the Holy Spirit. For He had not yet fallen on any of them; they had simply been baptized in the name of the Lord Jesus." Note: It is important to note that the Book of Acts is a transitional book between the gospels and the writings of Paul (between Judaism and Christianity). As a result, there will be different practices at different times. So, don't try to understand everything in the Book of Acts because you'll end up being confused. Believe me, even after many, many years of studying this book, I still don't get why there were many, different ways the believers in Jesus did things. I like how William MacDonald writes in his "Believer's

Bible Commentary: "They were all saved in the same way – by faith in the Lord Jesus Christ." So, I would recommend that, instead of trying to figure out who is doing what and when in the Book of Acts, try to look at the big picture and be thankful to God for how He worked through His people to bring people to faith in Christ.

In verse 17, Luke reports: "Then they (Peter and John) began laying their hands on them (the believers in Samaria) and they were receiving the Holy Spirit." Today, once a person becomes a believer in Jesus, the Holy Spirit comes to live within them immediately. Like I said, things were a little different back then in the early church.

Now, back to Simon. In verses 18 and 19, the good doctor writes, "Now when Simon (the magician) saw that the Spirit was bestowed through the laying on of the apostles' hands, he offered them money, saying, 'Give this authority to me as well, so that everyone on whom I lay my hands may receive the Holy Spirit." Can you see what Simon was doing? He only pretended to believe in Christ and followed the apostles around to see how they did their miracles. Then, he tried to buy the rights to the Holy Spirit to add it to his act, get his name back and prosper. Simon may have actually been the first "prosperity preacher." Sadly, there are many of them today who are making millions of dollars by preaching that God wants us all to be "healthy and wealthy!"

Now, you might remember, from the account of Ananias and Sapphira (Acts 5), that God sees everything, even our hearts and knows our motives. Peter, through the same Holy Spirit, saw right through Simon's scheme and said to him, in verses 20-23, "May your silver perish with you, because you thought you could obtain the gift of God with money! You have no part or portion in this matter, for your heart is not right before God. Therefore, repent of this wickedness of yours, and pray the Lord that, if possible the intention of your heart may be forgiven you. For I see that you are in the gall of bitterness and in the bondage of iniquity." In other words, he was still an unbeliever.

What was Simon's response to what Peter had said? Luke records in verse 24: "But Simon answered and said, 'Pray to the Lord for me yourselves, so that nothing of what you have said may come upon me.'"

You may remember, back in verse 13, Luke recorded, "Even Simon himself believed and was baptized." So, was he truly a believer in Jesus? William MacDonald calls him a "professor and not a possessor of true faith in Christ." I like that. Sadly, there are many of those still today who say they believe in Jesus, even His death, burial and resurrection, but then they also believe they need to be baptized, confirmed, take the sacraments and do other good deeds in order to be saved from their sins. Even at that, they still don't know for sure if they've ever done enough. Let me remind you what one of the greatest "do-gooders" of all time, Saul, who testified of his "do-gooding" in Philippians 3:1-8, but then said in Ephesians 2:8 and 9, "For by grace you have been saved through faith (in Christ); and that not of yourselves, it is the gift of God; not as a result of works, so that no one may boast."

Please know I am praying for all of you "do-gooders" out there for your salvation, that you will realize, as someone once told me: "It is not 'do, do, do; it's done" which Jesus proclaimed from the cross (John 19:30). Glory to God in the highest!

In verse 25, the good doctor reports, "So, when they (Peter, John and Philip) had solemnly testified and spoken the word of the Lord, they started back to Jerusalem, and were preaching the gospel to many villages of the Samaritans." Then, in verse 26, Luke writes, "But an angel of the Lord spoke to Philip (let's call him "Phil") saying, 'Get up and go south to the road that descends from Jerusalem to Gaza.'" I just love Phil's response in the first part of verse 27, "So he got up and went." Question: "Am I (are you) willing to go wherever the Lord leads me (you?)" We should be.

Next, Luke records: "There was an Ethiopian eunuch (let's call him "Ethio"), a court official of Candace, queen of the Ethiopians, who was in charge of all her treasure; and he had come to Jerusalem to worship, and he was returning and sitting in his chariot, and was reading the prophet Isaiah." Don't you just love all the details that Luke gives us about this Ethiopian?

Matthew Henry, in his Commentary, writes: "The Ethiopians were looked upon as the meanest and most despicable of the nations, as if nature had stigmatized them; yet the gospel is sent to them, and divine grace looks upon them."

We know, from John 3:16, "God so loved the world (that's everyone, regardless of skin color or nationality or religion) that He gave His only begotten Son that whoever believes in Him shall not perish, but have eternal life."

So, as Peter and John headed back to Jerusalem, an angel of the Lord sent Phil down a desert road to Gaza to meet up with Ethio who was probably a Jewish convert who had been worshiping in Jerusalem and was on his way back home.

Get this, Ethio is sitting in his chariot and reading the Book of Isaiah when the Holy Spirit says to Phil, "Go up and join this chariot." So, Phil runs up to the chariot and hears Ethio reading from Isaiah. In other words, he must have been reading out loud. Dr. Luke then tells us that Phil said to Ethio, "Do you understand what you are reading?" Great question! Maybe you're like Ethio; you read the Bible, but don't understand it. So, what do you do? The answer is found in Ephesians 4:11-16 where Paul writes:

"And He (Jesus) gave some as apostles, and some as prophets, and some as evangelists, and some as pastors and teachers, for the equipping of the saints for the work of service, to the building up of the body of Christ; until we all attain to the unity of the faith, and of the knowledge of the Son of God, to a mature man, to the measure of the stature which belongs to the fullness of Christ. As a result, we are no longer to be children, tossed here and there by waves and carried about by every wind of doctrine, by the trickery of men, by craftiness in deceitful scheming; but speaking the truth in love, we are to grow up in all aspects into Him Who is the head, even Christ, from whom the whole body, being fitted and held together by what every joint supplies, according to the proper working of each individual part, causes the growth of the body for the building up of itself in love."

I truly believe that the Lord Jesus has called and gifted me to be a pastor. Even though I feel as though I am done with being a fulltime pastor, I still believe I can be a "pastor-at-large" through supply preaching, writing books and a blog to help believers with understanding the Word of God and unbelievers with what they need to know about salvation.

Now, back to Ethio who then says to Phil in verse 31, "Well, how could I, unless someone guides me?" I just love what Luke records next: "And he (Ethio) invited Philip to come up and sit with him." Wow! Talk about an open door!

So, Phil gets into the chariot and discovers Ethio has been reading, of all passages, Isaiah 53, which is all about the future sufferings of the Messiah (Jesus) for our sins. Dr. Luke, then records Isaiah 53:7, 8 which says:

"He was led as a sheep to slaughter; and as a lamb before its shearer is silent, so He does not open His mouth. In humiliation His judgment was taken away; who will relate His generation? For His life is removed from the earth."

Ethio then asks Phil a question about the passage, "Please tell me, of whom does the prophet say this? Of himself or of someone else?" Wow! Wow! Wow! Door wide open for witness! Then we read, in verse 35, "Philip opened his mouth, and beginning from this Scripture he preached Jesus to him." Not only was Phil a great witness to Ethio, but also to us. He simply told this man about Jesus, His death, burial and resurrection which, according to Paul, in I Corinthians 15:1-4, is the gospel.

Now, granted, the Holy Spirit doesn't always speak to us and tell us who to witness to. But if we are available, then we need to heed what Peter said, in I Peter 3:15, "But in your hearts set apart Christ as Lord. Always be prepared to give an answer to everyone who asks you to give the reason for the hope that you have. But do this with gentleness and respect."

This, dear brothers and sisters in Christ, is a great example of when and how to witness of Christ. Notice, the Holy Spirit led Philip to the Ethiopian who just happened to be reading the Hebrew Scriptures and Isaiah 53 which is all about Jesus, His death on the cross for our sins, burial and resurrection from the dead. How cool was that!

Phil then explained the passage to him and, I am thinking, explained to him that he was a sinner who needed a Savior and as he believed in Jesus, his sins would be forgiven and he would have eternal life (John 3:16). Phil also must have told him something about believers' baptism. As soon as Ethio saw some water, he wanted to be baptized, as a symbol of identifying with Christ in His death, burial and resurrection. Again, I just love what the good doctor records next in verse 38, "They both went down into the water, Philip as well as the eunuch, he (Phil) baptized him (Ethio)." Note: We are not saved by baptism or any other sacrament or good work. But, when we believe in Christ as our Savior, we may then want to be baptized, identifying ourselves with Christ in His death, burial and resurrection.

What we read next is truly amazing. Luke writes: "When they came up out of the water, the Spirit of the Lord snatched Philip away; and the eunuch no longer saw him, but went on his way rejoicing. In the beautiful hymn, Amazing Grace," by John Newton, he wrote, "I once was lost, but now am found; was blind, but now I see!" Ethio once was lost in his sins, but now was found by Jesus; was blind but now could see the light and love of His Savior to the glory of God. One day, we'll get to see Ethio in heaven!

Oh, and one final note from the good doctor before we get to the next chapter. He writes in verse 40: "But Philip found himself at Azotus, and as he passed through he kept preaching the gospel to all the cities until he came to Caesarea." Azotus (today, Ashdod), according to "Nelson's Illustrated Encyclopedia of Bible Facts, was "one of the five chief Canaanite cities; the seat of the worship of the fish god Dagon; located halfway between present-day Joppa and Gaza." Certainly, Phil had his work cut out for him there. I look forward to meeting him one day and talking with him about it.

Act 9

Dr. Luke, in Act 9, records one of the most exciting and significant events in the history of the Church. You may remember, from Act 7:58, a man by the name of Saul was present when Stephen (the deacon turned evangelist) was stoned to death in verses 59-60). This would not be the only time he did this, as Saul testified before King Agrippa in Act 26:10, "Not only did I lock up many of the saints in prisons, having received authority from the chief priests, but also when they were being put to death I cast my vote against them."

After Stephen's death and burial, Luke records, in Act 8:3, "Saul began ravaging the church, entering house after house, and dragging off men and women, he would put them in prison." Later on, in two of Paul's own testimonies (Philippians 3:6 and Galatians 1:13), he described himself as "a persecutor of the church" and how he "persecuted the church of God beyond measure and tried to destroy it."

Let me pause for a bit and give you some

background on this Saul who was probably named after King Saul. We learn, from Acts 9:11, Saul was from Tarsus which, today, is in Turkey. In Philippians 3:5, 6, he tells us that he was "circumcised on the eighth day, of the nation of Israel, of the tribe of Benjamin, a Hebrew of Hebrews; as to Law, a Pharisee; as to zeal, a persecutor of the church; as to righteousness which is in the Law, found blameless." Here, Saul (now Paul) was telling us that he and his family were all about the Law and keeping it. Today, we call that "religion" which is all about what we do for God and not about what God has done for us in Christ.

Now, in case you've never heard this before how Saul became "Paul," Dr. Luke tells us in Act 9:1, "Now Saul, still breathing out threats and murder against the disciples of the Lord, went to the high priest, and asked for letters from him to the synagogues at Damascus, so that if he found any belonging to the "Way" (a name used for the church here and also in Acts 19:9, 23; 22:4; 24:14, 22, most likely based on John 14:6 where Jesus said, "I am the Way"), he might bring them bound to

Jerusalem."

As we shall see, the Lord had other plans for Saul. Dr. Luke tells us, in verses 3 and 4: "As he (Saul) was traveling, it happened that he was approaching Damascus (the capital of modern-day Syria), and suddenly a light from heaven flashed around him; and he fell to the ground and heard a voice saying to him, 'Saul, Saul, why are you persecuting Me?'" Note: When one is persecuting Christians, he or she is persecuting Christ Himself.

In verses 5 and 6, Saul responds to the voice, by asking a question, "Who are you, Lord?" The Lord Jesus responds, "I am Jesus whom you are persecuting." I like what William MacDonald says about this: "In order to appreciate Saul's emotions at this time, it is necessary to remember that he was convinced that Jesus of Nazareth was dead and buried in a Judean grave. Since the leader of the sect had been destroyed, all that was now necessary was to destroy his followers. Then the earth would be free of this scourge. Now with crushing force, Saul learns that Jesus is not dead at all, but that He has been raised from the dead." Luke then continues with Jesus saying to Saul, "but get up and enter the city, and it will be told you what you must do." Wow! The Lord Jesus has now taken a prisoner who just happened to be one of His fiercest enemies!

Luke then tells us in verse 7: "The men who traveled with him (Saul) stood speechless, hearing the voice but seeing no one." This made me think back to the time when Jesus spoke of His impending death in John 12:27-29, saying, "Now My soul is troubled; and what shall I say, 'Father, save Me from this hour? But for this purpose I came to this hour. Father, glorify Your name.' Then a voice came out of heaven: 'I have both glorified it, and will glorify it again.' So, the crowd of people who stood by and heard it were saying that it had thundered; others were saying, 'An angel has spoken to Him.'"

This also made me think of a future time in I Thessalonians 4:16, 17 where Paul wrote: "For the Lord Himself will descend with a shout, with the voice of the archangel and with the trumpet of God, and the dead in Christ will rise first. Then we who are alive and remain will be caught up (or raptured) together with them in the clouds to meet the Lord in the air, and so we shall always be with the Lord." So, I am thinking that when this happens, all the believers in Jesus, those who are dead and those who are alive, will hear a "shout, the voice of the archangel and the trumpet of God," while all the unbelievers on earth will either hear nothing or something else, like thunder.

As some of you know, I could go on and on about Bible prophecy, but that's for another day and, maybe even another book. Now back to Saul of Tarsus who has seen a light from heaven and heard a voice wanting to know why he has been persecuting Him, that is, Jesus Who then tells him to "get up and enter the city (Damascus), and it will be told you what you must do."

So, in verses 8 and 9, Luke records: "Saul got up from the ground, and though his eyes were open he could see nothing; and leading him by the hand, they brought him into

Damascus. You might say he was "blinded by the Light!" Luke then continues, "And he was three days without sight, and neither ate nor drank."

Then, in verse 10, the good doctor introduces us to a disciple of Jesus named Ananias (let's call him "Nias" so as not to confuse him with the Ananias of Act 5, although you may remember, he and his wife, Sapphira, were struck dead by God for lying to the Holy Spirit. This very much alive Ananias (Nias) received a vision from the Lord Who called him by name. I love his response which was very much like Isaiah's in Isaiah 6:8, "Here I am, Lord." What obedience! It was as if Nias was ready to do the Lord's bidding whatever that was, that is, until he found out what the Lord wanted him to do. My take on what Jesus said to Nias was: "I want you to lay hands on Saul that he might receive his sight." Nias was probably thinking something like, "I'd like to put my hands around his neck and squeeze really hard," explaining to the Lord: "Lord, I have heard from many about this man, how much harm he did to your saints in Jerusalem;

and here he has authority from the chief priests to bind all who call on Your name (including me)."

In verses 15 and 16, the Lord tries to reassure Nias saying to him, "Go, for he is a chosen instrument of Mine, to bear My name before the Gentiles and kings and the sons of Israel; for I will show him how much he must suffer for My name's sake." In a little bit, I'll show you some of what Saul (Paul) had to suffer for Christ.

What happens next gives me goosebumps every time I read it. Dr, Luke records in verse 17, "So Ananias [Nias] departed and entered the house, and after laying hands on him said, 'Brother Saul.'" Wow! Wow! Wow! This dear brother in Christ who was probably on Saul's hit list and feared meeting him, extends grace to him and greets him as a brother in Christ. I say, "Glory to God! Alleluia! Thank You, Jesus for not only saving a wretched sinner like me by Your grace, but showing me what that grace looks like through brother Nias!

Nias then tells Saul, in verse 17, "the Lord Jesus, who appeared to you on the road by which you were coming, has sent me so that you may regain your sight and be filled with the Holy Spirit." Get this, Dr. Luke records: "And immediately there fell from his eyes something like scales, and he regained his sight, and he got up and was baptized." Notice, Saul was baptized after he believed in the Lord Jesus. Later, in Romans 6:3-5, Saul turned Paul wrote about water baptism as "baptized into or being identified with Christ, His death, burial and resurrection." Let me say it again, baptism doesn't have anything to do with salvation as many, sadly, have believed and still believe today.

Dr. Luke concludes this section of Scripture by adding, "and he (Saul) took food and was strengthened. Then, the good doctor/historian adds: "Now for several days he was with the disciples who were at Damascus." Wow! Did you get that? These same disciples of Jesus whom Saul was going to arrest, bring to trial in Jerusalem and, maybe even vote to put them to death, were now his brothers and sisters in Christ! How cool was that!

Luke continues in verse 20, "and immediately he (Saul) began to proclaim Jesus in the synagogues, saying, 'He is the Son of God.'" Can this be the same Saul of Tarsus who cast his vote to have Stephen stoned to death for preaching that Jesus was "the Righteous One and the Son of Man standing at the right hand of God" in Acts 7:52 and 56? You betcha! One and the same.

So, what was the reaction of those who heard his preaching? Luke records in verse 21: "All those hearing him continued to be amazed, and were saying, 'Is this not he who in Jerusalem destroyed those who called on this name (Jesus), and who had come here for the purpose of bringing them bound before the chief priests?" Luke continues in verse 22, "But Saul kept increasing in strength and confounding the Jews who lived at Damascus by proving that this Jesus is the Christ."

In verse 23, Luke records, "When many days had elapsed, the Jews plotted to do away with him. In Galatians 1:17 and 18, Paul tells us he "went away to Arabia where he spent three years and returned once more to Damascus." Many commentators believe "the many days" are the "three years" Paul spent in training, probably with the Lord Jesus Who, I believe (and I could be wrong) trained him for the ministry, much like He did with the 12 apostles for the same amount of time.

Meanwhile, back at the ranch or Damascus, when the Jews tried to kill Saul, we read in verse 24, "their plot became known to Saul." This made me think of I John 4:4, "Greater is He that is in you than he that is in the world!" Now, that Saul had changed sides, Satan was not happy at all and tried to have him killed immediately. Because God is all-knowing and knows Satan's moves before he does anything, we are not surprised to read in verse 25: "They (his Jewish enemies) were also watching the gates day and night so that they might put him to death; but his (Saul's) disciples took him by night and let him down through an opening in the wall, lowering him in a large basket." Thank You, Jesus!

And, while Saul was able to escape harm and death this time, he would indeed have to "suffer much for Christ," as he records in II Corinthians 12:24-28: "Five times I received from the Jews thirty-nine lashes. Three times I was beaten with rods, once I was stoned, three times I was shipwrecked, a night and a day I have spent in the deep. I have been on frequent journeys, in danger from rivers, dangers from robbers, dangers from my countrymen (the Jews), dangers from the Gentiles, dangers in the city, dangers in the wilderness, dangers on the sea, dangers among false brethren, I have been in labor and hardship, through many sleepless nights, in hunger and thirst, often without food, in cold and exposure. Apart from such external things, there is the daily pressure on me of concern for all the churches."

It's no wonder the Lord brought the "beloved physician" alongside of him on some of his travels. Paul kind of makes me think of "Tim the tool-man Taylor" who was on a first name basis with those in the ER! Certainly, Tim gluing a board to his head does not even compare to what Paul went through!

Now, back to the story of Saul. Luke records in verse 26: "When he came to Jerusalem, he was trying to associate with the disciples; but they were afraid of him, not believing he was a disciple." That was certainly understandable for, one day, Saul was terrorizing the Church of Jesus Christ; the next, he's part of it. Barnabas then came to his rescue, as we read in verses 27, "But Barnabas took hold of him and brought him to the apostles and described to them how he had seen the Lord on the road (to Damascus), and that He had talked to him, and how at Damascus he had spoken boldly in the name of Jesus."

Dr. Luke then reports in verses 28-30: "And he (Saul) was with them, moving about freely in Jerusalem, speaking out boldly in the name of the Lord (amazing!). And he was talking with and arguing with the (unbelieving) Hellenistic Jews; but they were attempting to put him to death. But when the brethren learned of it, they brought him down to Caesarea and sent him away to Tarsus (his home town)."

What Luke records next, in verse 31, is also amazing: "So the church throughout all Judea and Galilee and Samaria enjoyed peace, being built up; and going on in the fear of the Lord and in the comfort of the Holy Spirit, it continued to increase." Can I get an "Amen" and a "Glory to God" to that? Thank you!

Act 9:32-12:19

Next, the good doctor tells us something about Peter's ministry in Acts 9:32-12:19 which contains a favorite passage of mine (12:1-19), the account of Peter being arrested and put into jail by King Herod after he had James the brother of John killed. This inspired me to write a poem called, "Twas the Night Before Pete's Trial." I recommend you read the Scripture account first, then the poem.

Twas the night before Pete's trial and all through the jail,
Not a creature was stirring, not even a snail.
Herod's guards put Peter in chains with much care,
In hopes that, by morning, their prisoner be there.

Old Herod was nestled all snug in his bed,
While visions of murder now danced in his head.
But Pete kept on sleeping in heavenly peace,
While the church was praying for his quick release.

When, all of a sudden, did an angel appear,
And a light filled the cell and made it quite clear
That he had come for Peter in answer to prayer,
To release him from jail as a sign of God's care.

Acting with Luke

The angel struck Peter to wake him from sleep
And said, "Get up quickly and don't make a peep!"
So, Peter got up, as his chains hit the ground
And put on his shoes without making a sound.

The angel told Peter to, "Come, follow me,"
Words he had heard Jesus say down by the Sea.
He followed him out, though he thought it a dream.
Passed one guard, then two, it was easy it seemed.

The iron gate opened mysteriously;
The angel departed, now Peter could see,
The Lord had rescued and saved him – good news,
But not for King Herod and all of the Jews.

Pete headed for Mary's, the mother of Mark,
Who had the church praying well into the dark.
He knocked at the door and the servant girl came,
She knew it was Peter, but left him just the same.

Rhoda got excited and ran to the church,
While Peter remained at the door in the lurch.
"It's Peter," she said, though they thought she was nuts,
She insisted, "it's him, no ifs, ands or buts!"

"It's his angel," they said and would not believe
God's answer to prayer they would not receive.
Peter kept knocking till they opened the door,
Then, they were stunned and almost fell to the floor!

They all got excited and made quite a noise;
Pete motioned for silence and said, "keep your poise!"
He told them the Lord had released him from jail
"Now, go tell James and the others without fail."

Peter then left Mary for another place,
While his guards had become an awful disgrace,
To Herod who ordered that they should be killed
If only he knew it was all that God willed.

The point of this poem is easy to see;
For God heard a prayer and rescued Petee.
So, brothers and sisters in Jesus, take heart
And trust Him by faith, right from the start!

When we get to Act 12:20-25, Dr. Luke tells us that, after Peter had escaped from prison and could not be found, Herod ordered the guards be executed. Next, we read at the end of verse 19, "Then he went down to Caesarea and was spending time there." In verse 20, we learn that Herod was not a "happy camper" with the people of Tyre and Sidon. To use an old expression, "while the cats are away, the mice will play." William MacDonald explains: "The people of these cities took advantage of his holiday in Caesarea to ingratiate themselves with him, because they depended on importing grain from Judea. So, they befriended Blastus, the king's personal aide and through him, requested restoration of diplomatic relations." What happens next is extraordinary.

Dr. Luke writes: in verses 21 and 22, "On an appointed day Herod, having put on his royal apparel, took his seat on the rostrum and began delivering an address to them (that is, the people of Tyre and Sidon). The people kept crying out (somewhat sarcastically I am thinking), the voice of god and not of a man!" Next Luke records, in verse 23, "And immediately an angel of the Lord struck him because he did not give God the glory, and he was eaten by worms and died." Yuck! Hmmm. Do you know anyone today who receives the praises of the people and has them bow down to him and kiss his ring as if he were God? I like how my favorite doctor/historian ends the chapter: "But the word of the Lord continued to grow and to be multiplied. And Barnabas and Saul returned from Jerusalem when they had fulfilled their mission, taking along with them John, who was also called Mark," the gospel writer and cousin of Barnabas.

Act 13

Now, back to "Acting with Luke" for another chapter or two before I finish this book. In Act 13, Dr. Luke tells us in verses 1 and 2, that Saul, Barnabas and three other men by the names of Simeon, Lucius and Manaen were fasting and praying in the church in Antioch. In typical Luke fashion, the good doctor/historian tells us a little more about each one, writing, Simeon was called Niger" which means "black." Charles Ryrie comments: "Niger was his Latin name and probably indicates that he was an African." Lucius was from Cyrene, a city in Libya, and Manaen, we are told, "had been brought up with Herod the tetrarch" which, despite what we might think, the Lord can and does save and work with politicians. Luke then tells us these men were at the church in Antioch, fasting and praying, when the Holy Spirit said to them, "Set apart for Me Barnabas and Saul for the work to which I have called them."

In verse 3, Luke records: "Then, when they had fasted and prayed and laid their hands on them, they sent them away" on what came to be known as "Paul's first missionary journey" which first took them to Salamis on the east end of the Island of Cyprus where "they began to proclaim the Word of God in the synagogues of the Jews." Now, "wait a minute," you might say, "I thought Saul was to be the "apostle to the Gentiles." Well, yes he was but, as we see in Romans 9:1-5, he had such a love for the Jewish people that God allowed him to tell them about Jesus on his way to the Gentiles.

Luke then adds, at the end of Act 13:5, "And they had John (Mark) as their helper." Later, in Colossians 4:10, we learn that John Mark was a cousin of Barnabas and, in Act 13:13, Luke records, "Now Saul and his companions put out to sea from Paphos and came to Perga in Pamphylia; but John left them and returned to Jerusalem which would later cause a strong disagreement between Paul and Barnabas which is for another book, Lord willing.

So, let me back up to Act 13:6 where Luke records: "When they (Paul, Barnabas and

John Mark) had gone through the whole island as far as Paphos, they found a magician. A Jewish false prophet whose name was Bar-Jesus (aka Elymas which means 'wise man,' which he wasn't). He was with the proconsul, Sergius Paulus whom Luke describes as "a man of intelligence, who summoned Barnabas and Saul to hear the Word of God."

As I have said before, whenever God is doing a work, Satan is usually nearby, ready to pounce "as a roaring lion seeking someone to devour" which Peter wrote about in I Peter 5:8. So, Luke tells us that this Elymas opposed Saul and Barnabas, "seeking to turn the proconsul away from the faith." Question: "Can you think of a time when the roaring lion tried to keep you away from the faith." I know I can. Now, listen to what happens next.

The good doctor wrote in verse 8: "But Saul, who was also known as Paul, filled with the Holy Spirit, fixed his gaze on him (hear it comes), and said, "You are full of all deceit and fraud, you son of the devil, you enemy of all righteousness, will you not cease to make crooked the straight ways of the Lord?" Pow! Paul's not done because in the next verse, he said: "Now, behold, the hand of the Lord is upon you, and you will be blind and not see the sun for some time." Another pow! Then, Luke records: "And immediately a mist and a darkness fell upon him, and he went about seeking those who would lead him by the hand." Strike three; you're out! And, guess what happened? Luke tells us, "Then the proconsul believed when he saw what had happened, being amazed at the teaching of the Lord." Glory to God! Hallelujah! Thank You, Jesus!

What happened next is something most of us, as Christians, either don't know about or take for granted. In Act 13:14, Luke records: "But going on from Perga (Asia Minor), they arrived at Pisidian Antioch (modern-day Turkey), and on the sabbath day they went into the synagogue and sat down." As far as we know, there were still no churches in these areas. Because of Paul's love for the Jews, he goes into the synagogue to witness. Notice the work of the Holy Spirit. Luke reports in verse 15: "After the reading of the Law and the

Prophets the synagogue officials sent to them, saying, 'Brethren, if you have any word of exhortation for the people, say it.'" Now, there's another open door! And Paul, recognizing the opportunity for witness, walked right through it and addressed the Jews, saying, "Men of Israel, and you who fear God, listen."

In verses 17-22, Paul then recalled for his fellow Jews their history from Moses to David. Then, in verse 23, he said: "From the descendants of this man (David), according to promise, God has brought to Israel a Savior, Jesus." No beating around the bush for Paul. He told them directly about the Savior, Jesus. Then, in verses 24-37, he spells out for them the gospel of the death, burial and resurrection of Christ. Next, in verse 38, he tells them boldly, "Therefore let it be known to you, brethren, that through Him (Jesus) forgiveness of sins is proclaimed to you, and through Him everyone who believes is freed from all things, from which you could not be freed through the Law of Moses." So, you might ask, "What was the purpose of the Law? Paul answers in Galatians 3:24, writing, "Therefore the Law has become our tutor (schoolmaster, KJV) to lead us to Christ, so that we might be justified by faith."

Think about it this way: God gave Israel the Ten Commandments (Exodus 20:1-17). Just the first one alone, "You shall have no other gods before Me," would do us in because if we are truly honest, we all, at times, worship someone or something else before God (parents, children, spouses, sports, movies, music, TV programs, computers, cell phones, tablets, jobs, hobbies, etc.). So, the Law was there to let us know what sin is and that, without a Savior, we are doomed to hell because we can never keep it perfectly.

Yet, because of God's great love for us and desire for us to spend an eternity with Him in heaven, He sent His Son, the Lord Jesus Christ, to the earth to die for our sins, that, as we believe in Him, His death, burial and resurrection, we would not perish in hell, but have eternal life in heaven (John 3:16). Glory to God! Hallelujah! Thank You, Jesus!

I just love what Luke tells us in verses 42

and 43: "As Paul and Barnabas were going out, the people kept begging that these things might be spoken to them the next Sabbath. Now when the meeting of the synagogue had broken up, many of the Jews and of the God-fearing proselytes (converts to Judaism) followed Paul and Barnabas, who, speaking to them, were urging them to continue in the grace of God."

Two of my favorite passages on grace are: Ephesians 2:8, 9 and II Corinthians 12:9 which tell us that we are saved by God's grace through faith in Christ and we are sustained by God's grace through all of our "thorns in the flesh."

When we get to verse 44, Luke records something amazing and thrilling: "The next Sabbath nearly the whole city assembled to hear the word of the Lord!" Wow! Wouldn't that be exciting today! As I have said before: wherever the Lord is doing a mighty work, the enemy (the devil) is nearby, waiting for an opportunity to mess it up. So, we read, in verse 45, "But when the Jews saw the crowds, they were filled with jealousy and began contradicting the things spoken by Paul, and were blaspheming."

Then, in verses 46 and 47, Dr. Luke records: "Paul and Barnabas spoke out boldly and said, 'It was necessary that the word of God be spoken to you first; since you repudiate it and judge yourselves unworthy of eternal life, behold, we are turning to the Gentiles." Then, they quoted from Habakkuk 1:5, "For so the Lord has commanded us, 'I have placed you as a light for the Gentiles, that you may bring salvation to the end of the earth.'" In other words, through Europe and across the sea to America and even to a place like Hartford, Wisconsin!

Luke then adds in verse 48: "When the Gentiles heard this, they began rejoicing and glorifying the word of the Lord; and as many as had been appointed to eternal life believed." Now, certainly, this sounds a lot like "election" or "predestination" and that God has already chosen a select number for salvation. I like what William MacDonald says about this:

"This verse is a simple statement of the sovereign election of God. It should be taken at its face value and believed. The Bible teaches definitely that God chose some before the foundation of the world to be in Christ. It teaches with equal emphasis that man is a free moral agent and that if he will accept Jesus Christ as Lord and Savior, he will be saved. Divine election and human responsibility are both scriptural truths, and neither should be emphasized at the expense of the other. While there seems to be a conflict between the two, this conflict exists only in the human mind, and not in the mind of God." I wholeheartedly agree!

The good doctor continues in verse 49, "And the word of the Lord was being spread through the whole region." This was certainly noticed by the enemy, as we read in verse 50: "But the Jews incited the devout women of prominence and the leading men of the city, and instigated a persecution against Paul and Barnabas, and drove them out of their district." What was their response? Just like Jesus said in Matthew 10:14, they "shook off the dust of their feet in protest against them and went to Iconium (Turkey)." Undeterred, we read, in verse 52, "And the disciples were continually filled with joy and the Holy Spirit. This brings me to the last chapter of this book.

Act 14

The chapter starts out in typical fashion: In verse 1, Paul and Barnabas are in the synagogue in Iconium preaching the gospel of the grace of God with a large number of both Jews and Greeks coming to faith in Christ. This was then followed, in verse 2, by opposition from both Jews and Gentiles. I just love the boldness in the next verse (3): "Therefore they (Paul and Barnabas or P&B) spent a long time there speaking boldly with reliance upon the Lord, who was testifying to the word of His grace (I just love that word), granting that signs and wonders be done by their hands." Charles Ryrie comments: "The miraculous signs and wonders confirmed the truthfulness of the message (II Corinthians 12:12)." Luke records the results in verse 4: "But the people of the city were divided; and some sided with the Jews, and some with the apostles." Sadly, today, a vast majority of people side with the enemy (the devil) and by comparison, a minority of those who side with the Lord Jesus, just like He said in Matthew 7:14.

In verse 5, we read that things got pretty intense for P&B, as we read of an attempt by both Jews and Gentiles to stone them to death. When they got wind of the plot, they left Iconium for the surrounding region where they kept on preaching the gospel (verses 6 and 7) and healed a man (verses 8-10) who was, get this, "lame from his mother's womb." I'm sure the good doctor was impressed again with the work of Dr. Jesus!

Interestingly enough, Dr. Luke records in verses 11 and 12, "When the crowds saw what Paul had done, they raised their voice, saying, in the Lycaonian language, 'The gods have come down to us.' And they began calling Barnabas, Zeus, and Paul, Hermes, because he was the chief speaker." In verses 13-17, when the people wanted to offer sacrifices to P&B, Luke tells us, "They tore their robes and rushed out into the crowd, crying out and saying, 'Men, why are you doing these things? We are also men of the same nature as you, and preach the gospel to you that you should turn from these vain things to a living God, Who made the heaven and the earth and the sea and all that is in them. In the generations gone by He permitted all the nations to go their own ways; and yet He did not leave Himself without witness, in that He did good and gave you rains from heaven and fruitful seasons, satisfying your hearts with food and gladness."

Sadly, despite Paul's message, Dr. Luke records in verse 18: "Even saying these things, with difficulty they restrained the crowds from offering sacrifice to them. Then, in verse 19, Satan goes for the jugular, as we read, "But the Jews came from Antioch and Iconium, and having won over the crowds, they stoned Paul and dragged him out of the city, supposing him to be dead." Despite Satan's efforts to take Paul out, we read in verse 20, "But while the disciples stood around him, he got up and entered the city." Did the disciples pray over him and he was brought back to life? Luke doesn't tell us. As someone once taught me, "Where God is silent, I must be silent too!" Whatever happened, praise God that Paul was still alive by the grace of God and, I'm sure, the care of Dr. Luke.

I like how Paul matter-of-factly ends verse 20: "The next day he (Paul) went away with Barnabas to Derbe!" Ho-hum; just another day in the Lord's work! Yeah, right!

Dr. Luke continues P&B's first missionary journey by writing in verses 21 and 22: "After they had preached the gospel to that city (Derbe) and had made many disciples (praise God!), they returned to Lystra and to Iconium and to Antioch (where they had started out from), strengthening the souls of the disciples, encouraging them to continue in the faith, saying, 'Through many tribulations we must enter the kingdom of God.'" This reminded me of what Jesus said to His disciples, in John 16:33b (and I like the King James Version translation), "In the world ye shall have tribulation: but be of good cheer; I have overcome the world."

Next, in verse 23, Dr. Luke records another important part of Paul and Barnabas' mission: "When they had appointed elders for them in every church, having prayed with fasting, they commended them to the Lord in whom they had believed." Every church should have elders, men of Christian character and a willingness to lead the church family. Paul gives us the credentials for elders (overseers) in I Timothy 3:1-7; 5:17-22; Titus 1:5-16.

In verses 24-26, the good doctor gives us the names of all the different cities P&B visited on their way back to Antioch: Pisidia, Pamphylia, Perga and Attalia. From there they sailed to Antioch, from which they had been commended to the grace of God for the work they had accomplished.

The good doctor then closes the chapter with these words from verses 27 and 28: "When they had arrived and gathered the church together, they began to report all the things that God had done with them and how He had opened a door of faith to the Gentiles. And they spent a long time with the disciples."

So, dear brothers and sisters in Christ, let me conclude this book by telling you that this Gentile is most thankful to God for the faith, witness and courage of Paul, Barnabas and my favorite gospel writer, Dr. Luke, who often sailed rough seas and walked along dangerous roads to bring us the Gospel, the good news of the death, burial and resurrection of Jesus Christ. May their long-suffering witness be an inspiration and encouragement to us as we watch, wait, work, witness and live holy lives for Jesus until He comes or calls us home.

For those of you who are not believers in Jesus, please know that God loves you and wants you also to spend an eternity with Him in heaven. Simply agree with Him you are a sinner who needs a Savior and that Jesus died on the cross for your sins, was buried and raised from the dead to forgive all your sins (past, present and future) and give you eternal life.

May God bless you all with faith or more faith in the Lord Jesus Christ to His glory. As I wait to see what the Lord has in store for me next, please feel free to follow my thoughts on my blog: dougsdailydoings.

Love in Him,

D. B. Livingston